the glory gets

WESLEYAN POETRY

Wesleyan University Press | Middletown, Connecticut

HONORÉE FANONNE JEFFERS

the glory gets

Wesleyan University Press
Middletown CT 06459
www.wesleyan.edu/wespress
© 2015 Honorée Fanonne Jeffers
All rights reserved
Manufactured in the United States of America
Designed by Mindy Basinger Hill
Typeset in Calluna

Library of Congress Cataloging-in-Publication Data

[Poetry. Selections]
The glory gets / Honorée Fanonne Jeffers.
        pages cm. — (Wesleyan Poetry series)
Includes bibliographical references.
ISBN 978-0-8195-7542-5 (cloth: alk. paper) —
ISBN 978-0-8195-7543-2 (ebook)
I. Title.
PS3560.E365A6 2015
811'54—dc23   2014043920

This project is supported in part by an award
from the National Endowment for the Arts.

5   4   3   2   1

FOR MISS LUCILLE

Out in the open wisdom calls aloud,

she raises her voice in the public square . . .

PROVERBS 1:20

CONTENTS

wit

fear

SINGING COUNTER

after Hayes and Mary Turner, Valdosta, Georgia, May 1918

The rope, the tree,
the tired comparison to Jesus on the Cross. Avoid the tropes.

The metaphors.
This stands for *that*, but if no one *black* ever says *that*, how would

someone *white* learn
this? How would any of *us*? I desire the surprise of intellectual,

fractured lyrics.
Yet here I am, refusing refusal. Calling the mob out by name.

Not even safely—
as with an anonymous *South*—but uncomfortably. As with *white*

man by *white* man.
(I'm scared just saying it.) And locating each in case

you have trouble.
(My People are exceedingly patient.) There: the expected

poor, drunk one,
neck darkened in the field. He's a nice cliché. But not the next:

a churchgoer
and father. A man who believes in Christ and the love of a virtuous

woman who fries
chicken for picnics and stirs up lemon cakes. After the lynching

he will continue
to believe and live his life in a good fashion. Beside him, his little boy,

smiling, his teeth
only beginning to loosen as he moves from baby to heir. He will grow,

remember his father's
beauty, the godly meat in that chest. In the back of this crowd,

a young scholar
home from college, brought by his friends who wanted to see

if what their science
professor said was true, that niggers did not feel pain the same

as better men.
Too old for the rowdy festival, someone's grandfather

remains at home.
An educated-in-the-North patrician who owns the newspaper

that later will run
the story. A savage raised his voice to a man. (One tenor

singing counter
to the other.) Or, he asked for his pay on Friday. Or, he

did not dance
when desired. Or, he did not step off the sidewalk for a lady.

(Should I explain
the Southern Anthropological Equation of *lady* plus *race?*)

Her flowered honor
required protecting. The imperative of her womanhood:

ax and gasoline
and black blood. Pig-like screams of what is not a man to the mob,

but a side
of meat. What never was in this place. I will admit these things

in my contemporary
time, but not out loud. My white friends and colleagues

(who are not
My People) would feel indicted by my saying, *I look at you and yes,*

I'm frightened.
I wonder if you would have sliced off my toe as I hung there, roasting over

the slowest fire
the mob could build. And later, killed my pregnant wife, the baby

still inside her.
I'm a sinner. I fear what I crave. Or love. Part of the falling,

the romance,
is a quandary keeping the present *here.* The past *there.*

A liquid-filled jar
of sex in a general store: before that day, its name was Hayes.

He made the mistake
of calling to her. Mary answered, her hand resting on her belly.

DRAFT OF AN EX-COLORED LETTER
SENT HOME FROM THE POST-RACE WAR FRONT

A soldier in Baldwin's Country & I can't even dance
        I say *you can't beat me*   Each day I get up to face fear

I made money & fixed my credit   I escaped you dear   my shame
        Yet how to escape white space   It's impossible

to return to your embrace   to rough-trading sweet vowels
        to brothers on corners visiting my dreams   I hear your whistles

smell collard greens on suburban wind   I love you with deception
        I'll be back   *I'll lift as I climb*   My remorse goes deep

to the whiteness in me   my bones   Forgive me   You don't know
        the trouble I see   I can't tell these folks the truth

They don't understand me & they don't try   Or try too hard
        I want my birthright   a mutual sight   my own ancient rime

In the bright trenches of the office   I open my mouth but choke
        on bottled water   Last week   I returned for your wake

but left before the Home-Going   I miss our surviving dark ones
        The familiar is trivial & profound   The strange a charge

in my blood   I clutch & shriek at these strangers I left drums for
        I sing B.B.'s mean old song

I END THE WINTER

Now is the winter of our discontent
Made glorious summer . . .
WILLIAM SHAKESPEARE

I end the winter,
discontented and frightened—
an evil child
facing the coming blues,
the weight of glory, of expectation.
This never-ending war.
Every blade I sharpen
is sure of its intentions.
This war and that—
every one God has commanded.
I'm speaking a true word—
when it's true that any bone
can explain why Samson carried
it into another's hinterland.
Them bones, hambones,
my-Lord-what-a-morning trombones—
oh please, come with me
to smite the weak.
I *know* that I know what God
knows, because He lives
in my scripture-singing self,
and since I command the babble
stirring the bricks of their tower,
I am made a godly God
and can piss oceans to replace
dead men's salt—
but if I were human, I would know this:
the soul has a body of its own
and will walk left or right.
The soul's flesh will turn,
its sweetness no longer nectar
but unbearable kindred.
This war today:
dry bones.

Fall in love with someone's poetry and thus, fall in love
with that someone. How many times can I explain this?
I'm running out of water. I'm not a child anymore.
        I'm talking to you.
I'm talking to myself, repeating a harpy's creation,
the chatter of disappointed women.
        Child, get yourself together.
I'm closing a book as my father's door was closed, as he locked
himself in a small room. This is not a metaphor. It was nearly a cell.
How did I know? Daily, I sneaked in there.
        He was gone.
The times he was present, maybe he was locked inside. I can't say
for sure. I can say what he forbade me: his presence.
        A knock at his black man's hour.
He had a soul. I know that. It was lined with the approximation
of tears. It was a hunger for scabs and scars. For life
to finally be over. He couldn't take his children and wife with him.
        He wrote so many poems.
I believe I've read them all. I read so many others. I've tapped the covers,
lifted a weight to my ear, hoping it would grow light in my hand.
        Congratulated the catharsis,
but catharsis isn't healing and my love isn't love. It's something else—
I'll get it together and I'll reopen the book. You'll reread this poem and fall
in love with me. Drive someplace I'm not. Cry one, two, three tears.

MY FATHER AS WALTER LEE YOUNGER

Here I am a giant—surrounded by ants! Ants who
can't even understand what it is the giant is talking about.
LORRAINE HANSBERRY

He is the giant.
We are the ants.
He wears the pants.
Remember, he wears the pants.

We are the ants.
We wear the smiles
of women in training.
Explaining to him

that we love him. Smiling
when now, the weather changes—
our sunny explanations
when his rage hails down.

Oh now, the weather changes,
so he's dancing mad and growing.
The ceiling hits his head.
The rage comes through the hole.

He is dancing mad, growing cold.
A daughter? Who cares?
Rage comes through his holes
as we quickly maypole 'round him.

Are you my daughter? he asks,
the nights he crawls the house.
Our minds blank, travel to spring
the nights he joins our beds.

The nights he crawls the house?
Here I am.
The nights he joins our beds?
Little ant.

Here I am: my father, my master
who wears the long pants.
I am his little ant.
He is the giant—

please, do remember that.

The mind pulls a sheet over the face,
the opaque mercy of zero memory—
the body won't return the favor. Though it

     sings glory

           to me

& the highest
crazy song

         i'm kicking

     it

worships at The Shrink's long couch,
its ear tuned to her calm leeching,

          with them

      other two

hands plucking at the full box
of paper handkerchiefs, the body

      this corporeal idiot

will ignore the mind's kindness,

         & our mistress
      we're in church
a field of scripture

           God is grabbing up dirt
    fertilizing sunflowers
       i know what comes

   next

          God will lift up my face

    for a slap &

instead suck the knowledge.
The mind will try to hide God's

            gift of knuckle

                        my body will fall

        on its back

               opening for the rack

     anonymous

                      male sacrilege

capricious taunting:

Daddy

              not my daddy

         night is daddy

                not my daddy

a cuckold, a thought, the two-timing,
alive entity and though unsatisfied
with life's slow-pouring mud, it dearly

loves puppies

            & kittens

                  &

                     la

la

        la

                la

beauty

MAMMY KNOW

after a half-plate daguerreotype of a slave woman
and her young charge, by Asa C. Partridge, c. 1840s

no paycheck in this year
this year black something is free

free   wine after Jesus rebuked water
water sweeter than milk

love in the hour before turning
turning   this body   this much

come back to a year
twice millennium

be still   auction block dues
due this woman   a charge's sharp teeth

teeth on the nipple
teat of Confederate need

need   let my people & her nipple go
go tell old Pharaoh to pay her

who knows the centuries' possibility
years of heirloom cat o' nines

whipping   humping a constructed tale
amnesia for sale   happy spayed slave cat

littered mother's milk   don't leave me
know me   (no me)

what Cause will rise
rise again   southern monuments

wench contentment & other lazy miracles
wonderful   the hands full of Daddy's whip

cruelty estate   frozen in a frieze   free
unchecked

PORTRAIT D'UNE NÉGRESSE

after a painting by Marie-Guilhemine Benoist, oil on canvas, c. 1800

I think,

I should emulate you: a pretty
bare breast suckling
Enlightenment, a quiet object,
subject of a logic's time.

I want,

need, to understand the tension
between fancy and pain,
but no one tells me
who captured

the aftermath,

how you went from
beloved to body:
a la Négresse—
face down, rump up,

free woman

remastered. When I see
your wrapped head,
gaze tentative, careful with your
remaindered modesty—

ma chère,

I wonder where your mama is.
Is she aware of this
moment? Would she
snatch you from

this pose

or push you to take bits
of sublime? Wherever
she is—
with you or across that water—

I've given

her the least I can.
Bewilderment. Reason.
I'm tired of beauty now,
these typical acts of light.

LIGHT

for and after Lucille Clifton

1. The House That She Built

Did not stand on a hill.
It was hidden behind
the trees of memory.

Inside were six children,
one husband,
one strong, weirding woman,

and fingers and fingers and fingers—
then the husband
and one son and one daughter

were gone, coaxed away
by candy and hymns.
I walked North toward a voice.

My woman was singing,
Here is freedom—
toss your quilt to catch it.

I stood outside
in a field far away.
I came and knocked at her door.

She opened and held out
a scarred knuckle that I grabbed
with one hand —

my other held onto my mother's.
Once I was a child unaware
of womanhood sneaking up

on me like rain.
I arrived at the truth
in her house today,

but before that,
I lied so nicely to myself.

This is my after-girl time,
the fire from the red
tree extinguished.

(No matter God's promises
there are ashes arranged
prettily on the ground.)

I walk through my house
naked on ordinary
days, slips and hips

on dramatic mornings.
I eat porridge for supper
and look about

for named objections.
None come.
No one claims me.

The grand love is absent
in the scripture's scheme,
my never-gone prayer.

It's a quiet
resentful time,
sometimes,

but a life, whether
that light is bright or dimmed
to every sinner but me.

3. She Left for the Party without Me

I can hear scattered roots
and new words at play.

I can hear a ghost
and spirits on this day.

They are going and coming,
each grabbing the other

on the way in and out
of this too-clean house.

The door opens and my old
lady curtseys to God.

I hear His saying,
You looking good, Lucille.

You gone steal the show.
My old lady stops to search

the mirror, fixing last
minute wrinkles.

Soon her girl will look back
when heaven has its way.

I try to follow.
I try to bar the door.

The spirits and the Lord ignore me.
My old lady says,

You wait here, baby.
I'll be right back.

I know she's jollying me along.
I'm ready to fight—

I can't stand when I'm mad
and nobody's home.

Moves forward
while someone moves
away from and to,

as in my people leaving behind
the frightening South
to enter the frightening North.

As in, I am shaking the dust
of this place off my clothes
and walking through that talking door.

Hey hobo, brother of my spirit,
make room there beside you,
if you please.

This train takes
you away,
maybe in the night—

I'm not sure of the time.
It writes poems as it is going,
to keep your journey light.

It calls out to Harriet,
We almost there, girl.
Y'all wait up for the rest.

It chugs for a Promised Land
where I can't follow.
It crosses some sorry,

grasping River Jordan,
bound for a heaven
I'm not sure I'll ever know.

I am angry,
but I suppose
I agree with this train.

blues

MAGDALENE BRINGS

Water: I wish him to be clean,
and next to a father's love.

Have you seen the man
You know where he's walking

Oil: he needs anointing,
as is seemly and right.

Have you seen the man
I heard tell he was here

Bread: he must eat.
Meat but no blood.

Have you seen the man
Peace done gone with him

Soon he will be passed down
a highway of tongues.

Have you seen my Jesus
Tell me   pretty please

MAGDALENE BEGINS
TO SEE JESUS

No seam joining
prophet to almighty—
river of blood,

secure and bright.
In the mud of vessels
cracks patched with spells.

Watching his face
take on doubt.
Call out to Him, I want to say.

Jesus, you taught me how.
Some things
he can't learn,

but if he asked a woman
I know he could be whole.
I ran from the soft

place I knew, came
here for apostles
to call me whore.

You think
I did that so he
could stand

a simple man?
Turn on his word—
the god he said he'd be?

WHAT JESUS SAID
TO MAGDALENE
AT THEIR LAST MEAL

I want a good death.
A peaceful escape.
Then dipped his bread,

shaking off excess.

His peace he leaves
by leaving me here.
And goodness—

but death? That's no gift.

And why men believe
women love to clean
house—

that we love suffering—

it's beyond me.
Times find a woman
left on the road,

her skin shouting bait.

I've traveled alone,
slept in the day,
hid with God at night.

I came to this life—

and now some *good death?*
I left his table growing cold,
his voice choking me.

Come back, my Magdalene—

Bread is good.
Water is good.
I wish he'd stop calling my name.

MAGDALENE'S WAIT

We prayed for death
to take him
His mother beside me
the other Mary screaming loud

She wouldn't stop
Oh   I wanted her to stop

We hoped those twelve
brothers would show
They scattered like rain
forgetting the day their god had made

When he cried out in thirst
& hollered *Daddy* & *Mama*
& *I don't deserve this*
& *See what they did to your baby boy*

When they stuck
that knife in his side
we prayed
& didn't it rain

& that woman wouldn't stop
God knows I wished she would stop

MAGDALENE
ON THE THIRD DAY

You are buried inside me,
a sharpening stone.
Five growing wounds.

That day,
I heard you weeping,
Father, take this away.

I waited, impatient
until you walked
one last time on dirt.

Were you God?
Were you Son?
Were you my lover

with eyes turned away?
No, a sky's breech birth,
crowned in discord.

Touch me not, you told me—
& then, I knew you for a man.

hoodoo

MEMORY OF A VISION
OF MARIE LAVEAU,
THE VOODOO QUEEN
OF NEW ORLEANS (1996)

A painting
of the Renaissance:

girl backed against a wall,
done over by the Holy Ghost.

Before those levees cracked open
I was supposed to drive

to the Crescent. Instead,
I built an altar topped by a china cup

and cheap bric-a-brac
in shades of blue.

Katrina's waters came and rose—
they're finally gone

and so are the graves.
What remains—

the lake and river innocent now—
never was blue,

and in that painting, Marie,
Queen of Salt-Tears,

the girl should be fat and brown.
No one can see the sound

of the drum
or understand she is unfaithful.

first i'm little   then i'm big   then the medicine come my way
then i'm red and black and a little dot of white   i try to find
the white till i stop trying   then i grow two new feet to match
my four feet kin   my name is deer   nothing else   just deer
call me that   i run till i reach the clearing   i shed my outside skin
i rear back on my legs   then the medicine come again   the medicine
take me over and i talk all out my head and my belly turn round
like water and the boat float in my blood and the people oh the people
they keep crying out to me   then the medicine take me over
and the boat women dance with me   then i put back on my skin
my four feet kin run away   then i cut off two feet but i don't bleed
and the medicine leave me cold and i'm little and i'm little
and i'm lonely and i'm screaming

ANGRY BLACK WOMAN
IN ROOT WORKER DRAG

after Oya

Some nights
      I love this earth to dust
            I shout umbilical prayers
            & they rise
      into tornado
I shake the spirit box
      surrounded by shards
            then fling back the scabs
            of houses
      Take my rivers
all of you
      & drink them
            I need no permission
            to drain
      the gourd
or split the hot
      yam center of dirt
            Yes
            my sacraments walk
      clothed in welts
but you don't have to believe
      In my throat
            the clutch of blood
            Take my rivers
      all of you
& drink them
      I tear
            & I tear open the breathless
            cradle packed
      tight

& blow the wall of wood
   sailing on my lifeline
     the nine streams of spit
     dammed by flying stone
   Now fall & call my name
a welcome for death
   & *Didn't my Lord deliver Daniel*
     is an empty pocket
     turned inside
  out

¹ The way you holler and call God's nine-one-one, wait for the Secret Poh-lice to come catch us. I'm grown: disobedience is a great beat-down. You can really dance to it.

² Ask the snake with a patch on his other eye.

³ And Gabriel, the high-C trumpet brother.

⁴ Woe is sassy me. *Surely and you, too, baby.* Woe is the Mule-Garden woman. *Okay, okay, now back to the Original Black Man.* Woe is my seventy-eight percent of the apple versus your whole got-damned tree. *I promise to be nice.* Walk over slow to me.

⁵ Let's move to atheist, dry foreplay on the kitchen table:

⁶ Du Bois is a bad-double-mother-shut-your-mouth.

⁷ Switch to trope role-play. You like that, don't you?

⁸ Yes, it's so hard when Big Daddy leaves you alone in broken-home Eden. Hard. The wide-open world. All you can do is pray on your knees:

⁹ But since your mama ain't my mama, can you please stop calling me sister? Can we skip the nasty incest and get right to the beast?

¹⁰ Leave the light on and let there be submission. Flip me over, authentic Eve-like. Stuff that fraction of an apple in my mouth.

¹¹ After, we'll read the Bible in the tub, and none of this will matter. Amen, awomen, and the river between:

¹² Chapter him and her and pink-in-the-middle rib.

¹³ Verse wiggling, hoodoo toes.

¹⁴ Praise and Noah cursing Ham with colored church. Greased rhythm, expectant sin, and unveiled ladies at the end-of-times.

¹⁵ Brown liquor getting you sure-enough lit.

JOB TO HIS DAUGHTER JEMIMA

The Lord blessed Job during the latter part of his life more than the former . . . He also had seven sons and three daughters. He named the first daughter Jemima . . . No one could find more beautiful women in the whole land than Job's daughters. Their father gave them estates together with their brothers.

JOB 42:12–15

any mother can describe
fear   pain
in your due time
holy can be unsteady
His love
a constant bloodiness
how foolish men are
but worship and praise
in this our duty
in a time after death
how capricious He is
forgive my ramblings
and oh how I love Him

the feral seed in a mouth
the many-called sufferings
be so afraid
a shouting outside
His joy makes me angry
a slant blessing indeed
I didn't deserve all that
how can I continue
you beloved and comely girl
you are nothing but a boon
in these insane days
and no I can't explain
how I remain His happy fool

Faith is a virgin wrist
is the dance only clay knows
is a lowercase prayer
the day's glare everlasting
Bark dressing the coy tree
and memory

I know a few things
but nothing past Sunday
Surely memory
was first   Lord   not darkness

If I could take You to task
I would ask that You
speak me to ashes   right now
unknit this flesh

Today You spoke to me
in the sacrament of coffee
and forbidden heavy cream
a steeple of jazz
the trumpet's squealing divinity

Your unseen hand revealing
a cupboard brimming with food

I live at the west end of Your eye
flood waters washing over
the eastern floor of someone's house
a tide of can't-hear-nobody-pray
I try to lift up a word
for them instead of swimming
in my own stupid miracles

My luck
ashé   amen
so it is with my life

Your will
for a few more days
until You won't

Before I came to You
I had a dream of a black
dog upon me   a demon
straining the length of silk
That dog chewed me
but I stayed closed to him

It was the devil that never sleeps
It was the sin
every woman keeps
tended if she is wise

And how does God come
to a woman
by a red trickle   by the fist
of a loved one held aloft
a benediction turned around
Omega before Alpha

a baby peaking out
of the friendliest place
she will ever know

There is only
a voice sliding inside
like thunder or a hungry man

I am foolish
following
what I cannot see
and so unfaithful to what
I touch

I should have stayed
in my house
and never come out
to greet this vale

I recall four words
You spoke

Before what was firmament
a sin cut in pieces   then joined
once more   crawling to life
A clay ball bouncing
blues in new high grass

After
You insisted it was good

There is some blessedness
each of us brings into a room
whether or not we sing
the praises of a named god

Allow me a breaking down

Hear me out before confusing
me with maddened masses
defining faith as blood and storm

I know I'm weak
I need something   a hope
for the chrysalis of Word
What won't take me
at my worst

This is spirit or medicine
The clasping of my hands
as I kneel before a rock
I am praying will speak

Look

I'm not trying to take anyone
away from this world

wit

THE GLORY GETS

for my replacement

The glory gets dingy quick.
Faking won't be as cute
as when he praised
your vast understanding,
but there's time before he hands
you cold cream
and whispers the truth.
Now, here's the key.
That window right there?
It sticks.
You have to pull real hard.
When you put away your shame
and reach outside to stroke
a shrinking globe, your hand
might shake, but give
thanks for small savoring.
You might consider that hunger
is prayer, and vice versa,
as our man should
before he quiets his mind
and rears back on his knees.
Claims the renewed place
he always assumed
he owned.
I didn't say he *would*.
I said he *should*,
but you'll find *should* can be
love if you sing
it just right.

FEMALE SURGERY

. . . let them think they have accepted
arrogance in the universe,
then bring them to gynecologists
not unlike themselves.
LUCILLE CLIFTON

Not by force.
        A *legitimate* violation.
        Oh, honey. Papers were signed.
Questions were traded.
        (Him: *May I approach you?*
        Me: *How much can you save?*)
Blood occupied,
        layers of fat and muscle cut
        through by his kind—
how to take a man to that place?
        No matter how fabulous
        the insurance,
there never can be trust.
        Try lying there, drugged up,
        the theatrical scene of counting
back from one hundred.
        Hoping to be that flawed
        animal surviving
a night in darkness.
        Waking up with staples
        barely holding in the guts,
leading down a now-flat road.
        When they slice the belly
        open like that, they discard
half of a woman and leave
        her the ovaries,
        perhaps
bits of the womb,
        the consolatory scar:
        the understanding lady

in the group
　　　　who'd closed her soft
　　　　surgeon's hand over the one
reached out to her.
　　　　Don't worry, girl.
　　　　You'll still get plenty wet.

MY 4:15 PM SHRINK'S
APPOINTMENT ON THURSDAY

Desire dogs me, though I beat her
with my walking stick.
Listen to my song, baby,
from a thousand kisses away:

Didn't you want me
I think you wanted me

I was too ready for you
to prove something—
ready and bold and quick,
though repeatedly, no luck.

Didn't you want me
I know you wanted me

Aching for your mean
laughter all up in my face.
Couldn't you have waited (decently)
for me to turn away?

Didn't you want me
Goddamn it, you wanted me

I don't care what
my therapist advised me yesterday.
I will not forgive
your forgetting of me,

you lowdown, too-sweet thing.
I will not stop calling.
I will not stop writing.
I just love these 4:15 blues.

I will not drive away
from this backwoods place.
Let's keep digging
these knee-deep graves.

MEMORY OF ONE DAY
IN A KITCHEN

It wasn't complete,
        only two hours
                I spent with you,
the light coy until evening—
        my rapid blinking,
                the way a girl did
once in a movie
        unworthy of the ticket's price.
                I felt so beautiful—
but then I called my mother
        and she made a noise when
                I said I could love you.
She was remembering
        Daddy—
                what she was wearing,
what he was wearing,
        each word they said,
                what everything meant
or would come to mean.
        In her alternate dreams, they
                hadn't married. She'd
taken the fellowship,
        studied overseas
                in France—
but don't get her *wrong*,
        she's *not bitter*.
                In fact, she's *perfectly fine*.
She didn't understand
        that I knew different:
                I'm one of the few,
good moments
        she shared with that pretty,
                redbone man.
She was thinking *blue dress*
        and *tweed jacket*
                and *1958*

when I said we sat at the table,
            speaking in hesitations.
                        Before we kissed
you took off your glasses,
            closed your eyes
                        while describing a moment
you wanted me to see.
            What if I'd reported my insanity to her?
                        That I'd bought condoms
for you.
            I was wearing
                        new panties.
I'd shaved the tenderness
            between my thighs,
                        but after you kissed me,
that was it. You left—
            I sat there,
                        the cork in the wine
bottle mocking
            me with its wistful,
                        funky smell.
It was a day of separation:
            the time before,
                        when a woman wouldn't
look for signs.
            The time after,
                        when a woman
could lose her mind,
            believe a note buried
                        in a man's laughter,
no matter what she says:
            Girl,
                        I'm through
with that sorry story.
            I'm way past all of that.

BIRTHRIGHT

Put me down easy, Janie, Ah'm a cracked plate.
ZORA NEALE HURSTON

After you are cleaned of your slick outfit,
you will scar down the seam of your mind
and grow tight-packed stones beneath your skin.
Nothing dissolves. No one will explain.
Daily you will search for real meaning
in constant death and sundry nonsense
but no meaning will take place—damn it.
You might give in and commence to pray
and God might visit and drink your tea,

but The Holy One won't stay for long—
you won't see whether this mystery
wears a flowered dress or tailored pants.
Your mother will give you her big pot
to stir, though you didn't ask for that.
She will tell you cooking heavy meals
will bring you immeasurable joy.
You will know she's telling you a lie.
You will cut your woman's eyes at her—

your enemy, another woman,
another convict, one more conflict.
You will hate her for pushing you through
her narrow door into a cramped room.
You will grow wise: your mother was born
only the day before you were born—
and no woman ever really dies.
You will thank her for her cooking pot—
gratitude, another betrayal.

PATIENCE

Springplace Plantation, Georgia, c. 1811

Must these stories sound the same?—

a trader's march from South Carolina,
coffle train in freezing weather.
Patience the name of the slave

who crawled, her feet loved off by frostbite.

And should I ask the questions:
could she see this place today,
the blank, sinless text?

Memory. History. Dirt. (Not in the least.)

I'd think of her on my walk
back to my sunlit home,
but what of my selfish hands fastened

on the plow of a supposedly better day?

My understanding of her unfree
God seizures, her praise
in spite of no blessings?

What on this earth did she anticipate,

a crippled woman bolstered by grace?
And what of this aging task before me,
a chorus of *that was then*?

I could give you *Patience*, a place to make holy

and save for a given day.
Demand that you share my load—
why don't *you* carry her for a while?

You expect that from me.

I expect it from myself—
a sorrow-song prospect—
so reject the inevitable: don't

carry her, on your back or in your hands.

Don't even think about *Patience*.
Forget this woman,
if you can.

IF FREE, THEN

after Wallace Stevens and
Raymond R. Patterson

1.

A woman is a bird:
Birdy Black.
A patched being
against sky and earth.

2.

Birdy rises early
with no consolation.
Not even a measly worm.

3.

The swelled knuckles
of Birdy's hands.

This time, arthritis.
Next, *Child,*
you better move.

4.

Once, Birdy thought
she might fly back
over the water.
She discovered no
translation for wings.

5.

Birdy decides to love
herself and talk
about it in public.
Birdy is called *angry*.
Birdy is called *ungrateful*.
Birdy is called *object*.
Birdy and Zora
become best friends.

6.

Birdy Black
is a woman.
Now add to that,
Birdy Black is
a black woman.
Now see her.
What does that equal?

7.

Does anyone
know Birdy's age?

Smooth skin:
reparations for slavery.

8.

Birdy.
Sky.
God.
Jesus.
Sky again.
Birdy, meet Bird.
Jazz.

9.

Birdy reads a book.
The book speaks of water,
of slavery, of earth,
of bad, loud women.

Do you know me?
Birdy asks that book,
which has started talking.

Yes, it replies.
*I knew you before
you were born.*

10.

Come day, Sunday:
for God so loved woman,
He called her Birdy.

Then, He bade her
to fry chicken.

11.

World is world.
Life is life.
Birdy is here to stay,
alive or dead.
There is need
for complaint,
but no supplication.

12.

Given:
if Birdy, then free.

If free, then singing.

Thus, the Gospel
of Birdy.

13.

Soon one morning—
song done,
and here morning be.

Birdy in the wind.

"Singing Counter" is based on my reading about the murders of Hayes and Mary Turner and their eight months' unborn child in Phillip Dray's *At the Hands of Persons Unknown: The Lynching of Black America* (2007). I read further on this horrific event in Julie Buckner Armstrong's *Mary Turner and the Memory of Lynching* (2011). My poem is not an exact, historical rendering of this triple homicide, but rather an imagining of an event like it.

"Draft of an Ex-Colored Letter Sent Home from the Post-Race War Front" is written after James Weldon Johnson's *The Autobiography of an Ex-Colored Man* (1912).

"Portrait D'une Négresse." This poem contains a reference to a sexual position, "Négresse," included in the original edition of Alex Comfort's *The Joy of Sex: A Gourmet Guide to Love Making* (1972). According to Comfort's description, this woman—ostensibly of African descent, as indicated by the name of the position—lies face down in a submissive pose, the entire front of her body hidden from her partner.

"Light" is dedicated to Lucille Clifton and owes a great artistic debt to *Good Woman: Poems and a Memoir 1969–1980* (1987). In particular, "4. The Train Bound for Glory" is written after "the lesson of the falling leaves" found within *Good Woman*.

"Patience." I am grateful to the guides at the Chief Vann Springplace Plantation in North Georgia for pointing me to the story of Patience, whom I read about further in Rowena McClinton's two edited volumes of *The Moravian Springplace Mission to the Cherokees* (2007).

"If Free, Then" is written after Wallace Stevens's "Thirteen Ways of Looking at a Blackbird" from *Harmonium* (1923), and Raymond R. Patterson's "Twenty-Six Ways of Looking at a Black Man" from *Twenty-Six Ways of Looking at a Black Man and Other Poems* (1969).

GRATITUDE

First, as always, I give unashamed glory and praise to a mighty God from Whom all blessings, words, and wisdom flow.

I give gratitude to the ancestors for watching over me, especially Lucille Clifton, who was my rock for eleven years and who saved me in so many ways. Her passing left a hole in the black writing community—and in my heart—that will never be filled. I hope to see you on the other side, Miss Lucille. I'm sending up my timber.

The good-woman guidance of my mother, Trellie James Jeffers, offers me more than words can convey.

Beloved mentors Jerry Ward, Jr., Afaa Michael Weaver, and Hank Lazer, thank you for your continual beliefs in my abilities as a writer, intellectual, and human being over all these years. I live to make you proud.

I'm indebted to those who kept me going through the writing of this book: James William Richardson, Jr., Crystal Wilkinson, Andrea Franckowiak, Remica L. Bingham-Risher, Andrew Jeon, Cherise Pollard, Herman Beavers, Anthony Walton, Lynette Leidner, and Tony Medina.

Appreciation and admiration to Rita Dove, Natasha Trethewey, Elizabeth Alexander, Joanna Brooks, Cyrus Cassells, David Lynn, Maggie Anderson, Sonia Sanchez, Quincy Troupe, D. A. Powell, and Geary Hobson.

To my dear husband, Idrissa Diakhaté, sama djeker bueguenala.

Boundless thanks to Kwame Dawes, A. Van Jordon, and Tracy K. Smith.

PUBLICATION ACKNOWLEDGMENTS AND CREDITS

Grateful acknowledgement to the following publications for featuring my poems, some in earlier forms with different titles:

A Joint Called Pauline, "My 4:15pm Shrink's Appointment on Thursday" (first appeared as "What My Therapist Told Me").
Alehouse Review, [Faith is a virgin wrist].
Black Renaissance Noire, "Draft of an Ex-Colored Letter Sent Home from the Post-Race War Front."
Cavalier Literary Couture, "Portrait D'une Négresse" (first appeared as "La Négresse").
Connotations Press Online, [There is some blessedness].
Georgetown Review, "Patience."
Iowa Review, "Singing Counter," "Mammy Know," and "Try to Hide."
Lo-Ball, "Apologia for Something."
Obsidian III: Black Literature in Review, "Angry Black Woman in Root Worker Drag" (first appeared as "Oya's Rage").
Tidal Basin Review, "After, We'll Read the Bible" and "If Free, Then."
Yellow Medicine Review: A Journal of Indigenous Literature, Art and Thought, "I End the Winter," "The Glory Gets" (first appeared as "Instructions to my Replacement"), "Memory of a Vision of Marie Laveau, the Voodoo Queen of New Orleans (1996)," and "Memory of an Ancestral Vision (2006)."

Excerpt from *Richard III* by William Shakespeare.

Excerpt(s) from *A Raisin in the Sun* by Lorraine Hansberry, copyright © 1958 by Robert Nemiroff, as an unpublished work. Copyright © 1959, 1966, 1984 by Robert Nemiroff. Copyright renewed 1986, 1987 by Robert Nemiroff. Used by permission of Random House, an imprint and division of Random House LLC. All rights reserved. All third-party use of this use of this material, outside this publication, is prohibited. Please contact Random House LLC for permission.

ABOUT THE AUTHOR

Honorée Fanonne Jeffers is the author of three previous books of poetry: *The Gospel of Barbecue*, *Outlandish Blues*, and *Red Clay Suite*. Her poems have appeared widely in anthologies and journals such as *Angles of Ascent: A Norton Anthology of Contemporary African American Poetry*, *Kenyon Review*, and *Iowa Review*. She is an associate professor of English at the University of Oklahoma.